LEARN ABOUT PAGANISM

Beltane

WITH

Grani Hulda

Pagan Books for Pagan Kids

Grani Hulda

This book belongs to:

_____

2022 Grani Hulda

What is Beltane?

Beltane is the time of year when the Earth energies are at their strongest.

Beltane is celebrated mid-way between Spring and Summer, at the peak of Spring when all life is blooming.

The Oak King is getting strong at Beltane.

Beltane lets us know that Summer is almost here. The weather changes a lot. It is sometimes rainy and sometimes sunny.

Grani Hulda's garden is starting to grow.

Everything in Nature is growing and buzzing with life.

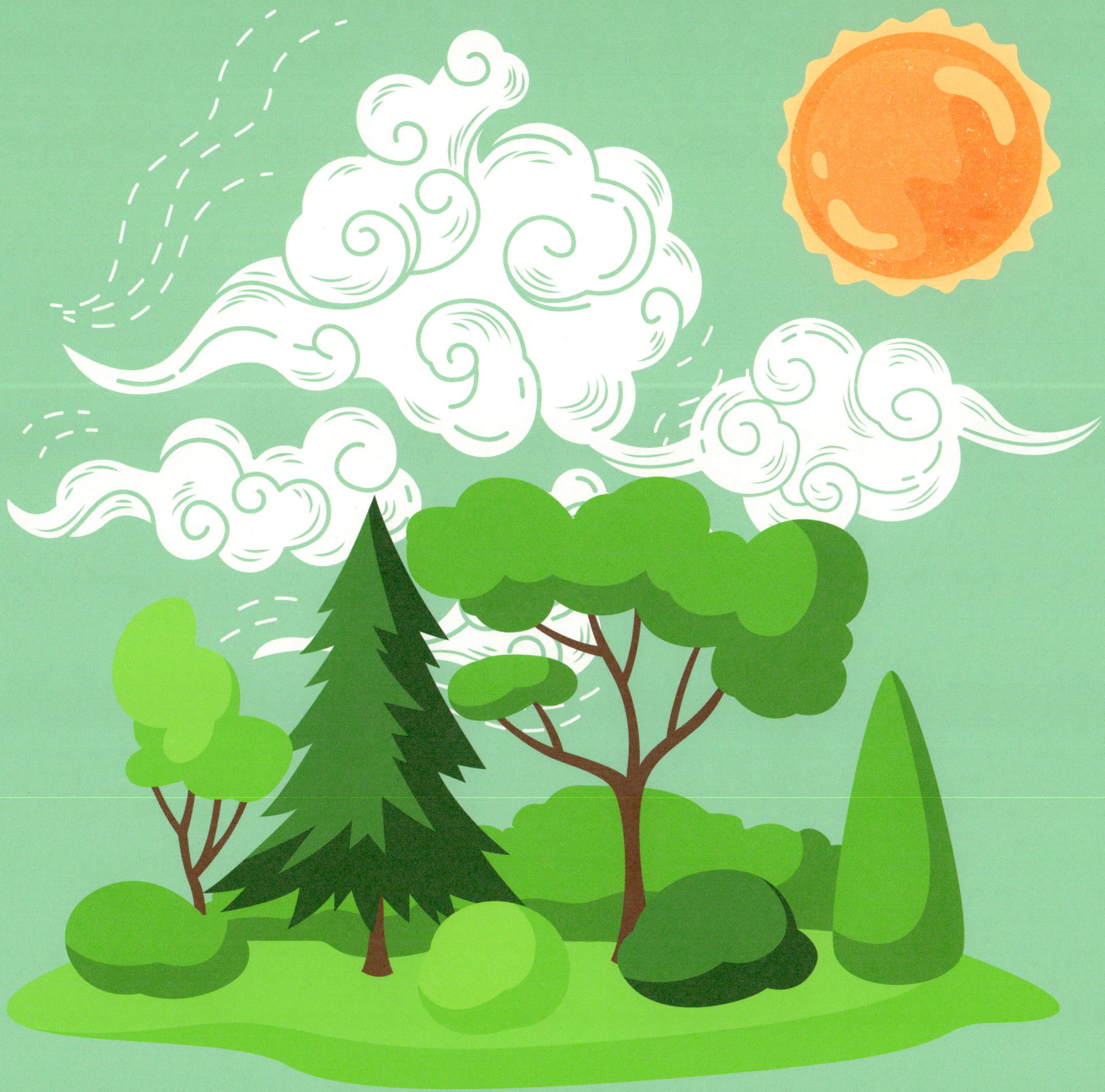

The Fae Folk

The Fae folk are active at Beltane.

Three black coals placed under a butter churn will keep fairies away from the butter.

Place flowers on your doorstep to keep the fairies happy. They love the nectar from the flowers, just like bees and hummingbirds do!

Fairies also like songs and poems, especially when they are written just for them. Grani Hulda likes to write poems for all of the Fae Folk at Beltane.

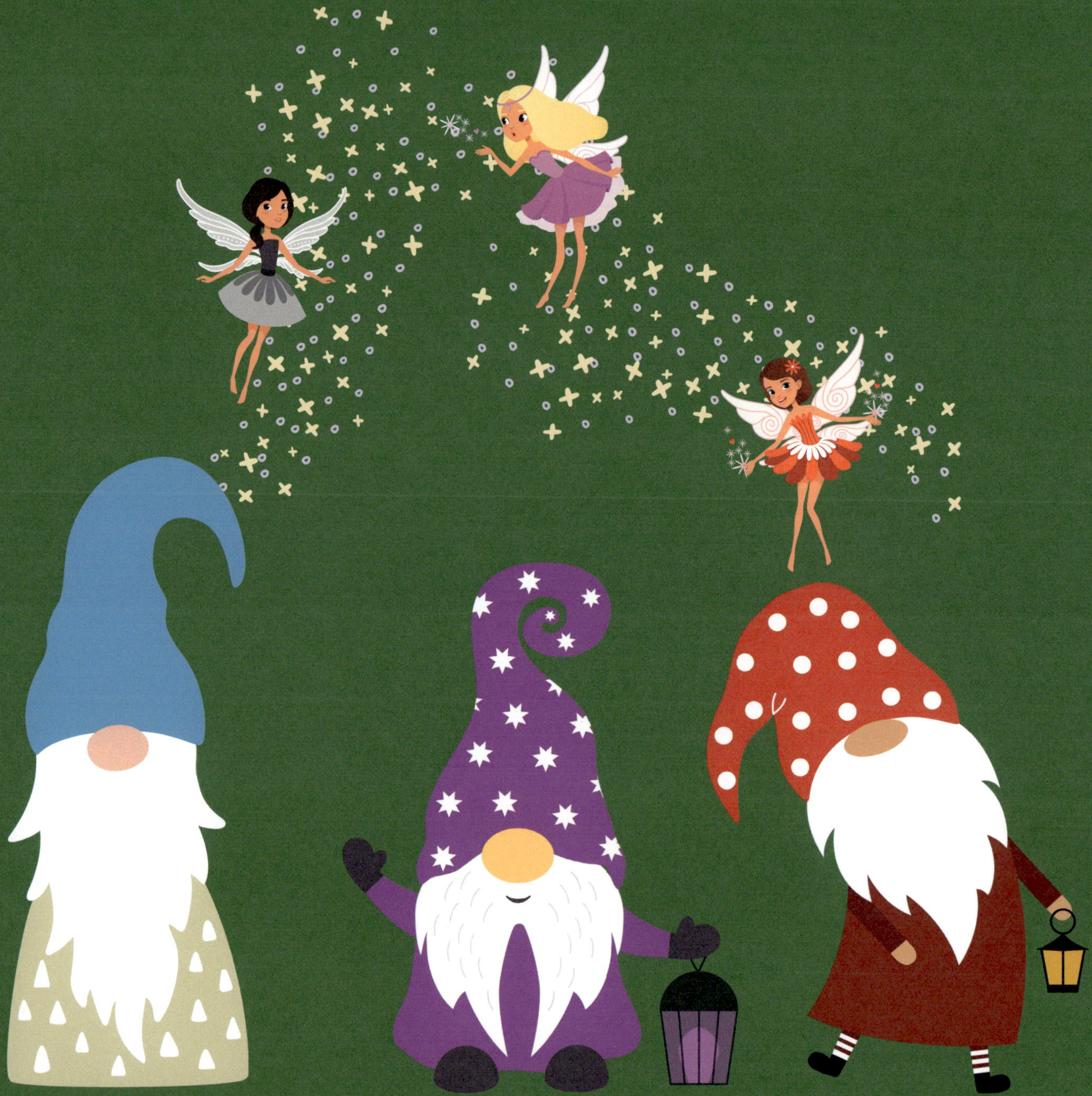

Celebrate Beltane

There are many ways to celebrate Beltane.

Make a flower crown to celebrate Beltane. Our ancestors used to make flower crowns for their cows.

A Maypole is a common way to celebrate Beltane with friends and family.

Grani Hulda likes to have a fire at all of the Sabbats.

You can also decorate a May Bush at Beltane to bring good luck to your home.

Leave offerings like coins or special rocks at a holy well or river near your home to create abundance for your family.

Celebrate Beltane by noticing the colors and sounds in the world around you.

The Earth even smells different at Beltane. Taking a walk in Nature is a good way to celebrate Beltane.

Smell the air. Look at the trees. Listen to the birds. Enjoy the Sun.

Happy Beltane!

Made in the USA
Columbia, SC
20 April 2025